Fundamental Tax Reform and Corporate Finance

Fundamental Tax Reform and Corporate Finance

William M. Gentry and R. Glenn Hubbard

The AEI Press

Publisher for the American Enterprise Institute
WASHINGTON, D.C.
1997

*We are grateful to David Bradford, Robert Hall, and partici-
pants in the NBER Conference "Asset Price and Transition
Effects of Consumption Tax Reform" and the NYU Tax Policy
Colloquium for comments and suggestions, and to James
Combs for excellent research assistance.*

W.M.G. and R.G. H.

*A slightly different version of this text will appear in the
NBER's Tax Policy and the Economy series, to be published
by the MIT Press.*

Distributed to the Trade by National Book Network, 15200 NBN Way,
Blue Ridge Summit, PA 17214. To order call toll free 1-800-462-6420 or
1-717-794-3800. For all other inquiries please contact the AEI Press, 1150
Seventeenth Street, N.W., Washington, D.C. 20036 or call 1-800-862-5801.

ISBN 0-8447-7085-X   ISBN 978-0-8447-7085-7

1 3 5 7 9 10 8 6 4 2

THE AEI PRESS
Publisher for the American Enterprise Institute
1150 17th Street, N.W., Washington, D.C. 20036

Contents

Foreword

Economists, policy makers, and business executives are keenly interested in fundamental tax reform. High marginal tax rates, complex tax provisions, disincentives for saving and investment, and solvency problems in the social security program provide reasons to contemplate how reforms of the tax code and other public policies toward saving and investment might increase economic efficiency, simplify the tax code, and enhance fairness. Many economists believe that gains to the economy from an overhaul of the income tax or from a move to a broad-based consumption tax can be measured in the trillions of dollars. Most conventional economic models indicate a potential for large gains from tax reform.

While many economists agree broadly on the simple analytics of tax reform, they are in much less agreement on such key empirical questions as how much saving or investment would rise in response to a switch to a consumption tax, how much capital accumulation would increase under a partial privatization of social security, how reform would affect the distribution of taxes, and how international capital markets influence the effects of tax reforms in the United States. This lack of professional consensus has made the policy debate fuzzy and confusing.

With these concerns in mind, Diana Furchtgott-Roth and I organized a tax reform seminar series at the American Enterprise Institute beginning in January 1996. At each seminar, an economist presented new empirical research on topics relating to fundamental tax reform. These topics include transition problems in moving to a consumption tax, the effect of taxation on household saving, distributional effects of consumption taxes in the long and short run, issues in the taxation of financial services, privatizing social security as a fundamental tax reform, international issues in consumption taxation, distributional consequences of reductions in the capital gains tax, effects of tax reform on pension saving and nonpension saving, effects of tax reform on labor supply, consequences of tax reform on business investment, and likely prototypes for fundamental tax reform.

The goal of the pamphlet series in fundamental tax reform is to distribute research on economic issues in tax reform to a broad audience. Each study in the series reflects many insightful comments by seminar participants—economists, attorneys, accountants, and journalists in the tax policy community. Diana and I are especially grateful to the two discussants of each paper, who offered the perspectives of an economist and an attorney.

I would like to thank the American Enterprise Institute for providing financial support for the seminar series and pamphlet series.

R. GLENN HUBBARD
Columbia University

1
Introduction

One of the most complex areas of the U. S. tax system is the treatment of business financing and investment decisions. Much of the complexity arises because managers try to minimize their firms' tax liability through tax planning. These tax-planning strategies could differ substantially if the United States undertakes a fundamental tax reform. In this volume, we describe the major effects of fundamental tax reform on corporate financial policy and summarize economists' knowledge of the magnitude of these different effects. We concentrate on financial policy issues rather than on the effects of fundamental tax reform on aggregate saving and investment, which are often cited as an impetus for reform (see, for example, the analysis in Auerbach 1996).

We identify four major areas of policy concern. First, in the short run, tax reform could cause changes in asset values by changing the relative tax treatment of existing and new investment. Such changes could create substantial windfall gains and losses to owners of specific assets. Second, tax reform could affect decisions on business organization and reorganization. Third, fundamental tax reform could influence firms' decisions on capital structure—the choices between debt and equity financing and between dividends and retained earnings. Fourth, fundamental tax reform could greatly alter the tax-planning landscape, which would affect the complex financial transactions (derivatives and swap contracts, for example) that firms use to lower their tax payments under current tax rules.

Fundamental tax reform is a broad term that encompasses a wide range of policies, including income tax reforms and replacing the current tax system with a broad-based consumption tax. Despite this range of policies, possible reforms have several common features. First, a common goal of tax reforms is to reduce the disparity in tax rates across different types of real assets and across different financial contracts. Second, fundamental tax reforms of both the income and the consumption variety typically call for a broad tax base with lower marginal tax rates. For income tax reform, our definition of fundamental tax reform includes proposals to integrate the personal and corporate tax systems and move toward a more consistent definition of income across types of assets. Moving to a consumption tax can be thought of as taking such an income tax reform one step further—the consumption tax would replace the system of depreciation allowances under the integrated income tax with immediate deductions for capital outlays of businesses. Because the two reforms share this first step, many of their effects on corporate finance are similar.[1] For the issues we consider, however, the administrative feasibility of the consumption tax may have advantages over income tax reform.

This volume proceeds as follows. Chapter 2 briefly outlines prototypes for tax reform and their treatment of the business sector and financial assets. Chapter 3 discusses how the transition to a new tax system could affect the relative valuation of assets. Depending on the transition rules included in tax reform, these asset valuation effects could be larger for moving to a consumption tax rather than income tax reform. The key issue for the valuation effects is whether the rules governing the transition to a consumption tax would disallow depreciation allowances expected on current assets. In chapter 4, we discuss the potential effects of tax reform on the organizational form of businesses, the source of finance, and payout policy. Chapter 5 discusses how fundamental tax reform would affect tax planning by businesses, especially with respect to their use of complex financial transactions. Chapter 6 summarizes our findings.

2
Prototypes for Fundamental Tax Reform

T he current U.S. tax system is a hybrid of income and consumption tax rules (see, for example, the review in Engen and Gale 1996). The reasons behind the hybrid tax system include both administrative issues (for example, difficulties in measuring income accruing as unrealized capital gains or as consumption flows from consumer-owned durables) and policy choices (for example, special tax provisions for retirement saving). Proposals for fundamental tax reform typically suggest moving to either a purer income tax or a purer consumption tax. Although these two "goals" appear to be on opposite ends of a spectrum, the purer income tax and the purer consumption tax may affect corporate financing decisions in similar ways. Moving to a purer tax system of either type would reduce tax-planning opportunities because tax-minimizing strategies often involve combining transactions with different tax treatments (for instance, part of the transaction receives pure income tax treatment, but another part receives consumption tax treatment) or taking advantage of disparities in tax rates across investors.

In the next section, we describe a prototype of income tax reform. We proceed to show how this income tax could be converted into a consumption tax and argue that this conversion would not have major implications for corporate finance issues. We conclude the chapter with a brief discussion of how some of the policy choices in the proto-type reforms affect the possibilities for tax planning.

Broad-based Income Tax Reform

For corporate finance, the critical element of fundamental reform of the income tax is the integration of the corporate and the personal income tax systems. In theory, integrating the systems would eliminate two distortions from the current tax system. First, integrating them would erase the distinction between corporate and noncorporate businesses by abolishing the double taxation of equity-financed corporate taxation. Second, this reform would remove the differential taxation of debt and equity finance. Whether the actual tax reform process would deliver these benefits depends on the details of the new system.

The U.S. Treasury Department's recent study of corporate tax integration (see U.S. Department of the Treasury 1992) presents several alternative approaches to integrating the individual and corporate tax systems. Rather than repeat this discussion of the many different proposals, we outline a stylized version of one proposal, the comprehensive business income tax (CBIT). The goal of CBIT is to tax business income once. CBIT is a business-level tax on the return to capital of businesses. Broadly speaking, the business-level tax base under CBIT is revenue from the sale of goods or real assets less wages, material costs, and depreciation allowances for capital investments. To conform to standard income accounting, the CBIT tax base uses depreciation allowances that follow as closely as possible economic depreciation. Because CBIT is a tax on capital income, it runs afoul of the standard income tax accounting problem of adjusting for inflation. If the government wants to tax real, rather than nominal, capital income, the cost recovery system (depreciation allowances) must be indexed for inflation. CBIT does not distinguish whether capital is financed by borrowing or by issuing equity. That is, relative to the current tax system, CBIT would not allow businesses to deduct interest payments from their tax base.[2] Because CBIT taxes business income at the entity level, there is no need for investor-level taxes on capital gains, interest, or dividends received.[3]

CBIT can be thought of as the capital income tax component of a broad-based income tax that collects taxes from labor income through a tax on household wages. We assume, for simplicity, that the marginal tax rate in CBIT is the same as the marginal rate for wage taxes. With this assumption, capital and labor income face the same tax rate. If the wage tax rate differs from the CBIT rate, then labor and capital income face different tax rates; however, capital income from different types of assets faces a common tax rate regardless of whether it is financed by debt or by equity.[4]

Converting the Income Tax into a Consumption Tax

Converting CBIT into a consumption tax turns out to be quite straightforward. Instead of measuring business income through depreciation allowances, a consumption tax version of CBIT would allow businesses a deduction for capital investments when assets are purchased. This adjustment converts the combination of CBIT and a wage tax into the flat tax proposed by Hall and Rabushka (1983, 1995). We use the flat tax as the model of the consumption tax for the purposes of this book.[5] Our focus on expensing as the central difference between CBIT and the flat tax reflects our emphasis on the effects of tax reform on business finance. The flat tax has an added advantage of mitigating the distortions of capital allocation between the business and the housing sectors. In the aggregate, the tax base is a measure of consumption because sales between businesses induce offsetting inclusions and deductions for the seller and buyer: the seller's tax base increases by the purchase price, but the buyer's tax base decreases by the purchase price. If the buyer and seller face the same tax rate, then the transaction creates no revenue for the government. When a business sells goods to households, the aggregate tax base increases by the value of the purchase.

Having described CBIT and the flat tax in this way, we can see that the flat tax does not exempt all of what is commonly called "capital income" from taxation (see also Gentry and Hubbard 1997). Under the business cash-flow tax component of the flat tax, the present value of depreciation allowances for one dollar of current investment is one dollar, while the present value is less than one dollar under the income tax. For a risk-free investment project, the tax savings from depreciation allowances represent risk-free flows,[6] which the firm would discount at the risk-free rate of interest. For a marginal investment (in which the expected rate of return just equals the discount rate), the upfront subsidy to investment provided by expensing equals the expected future tax payments. It is in this sense that the "return to capital" is not taxed under a cash-flow tax or a consumption tax.[7]

What about inframarginal investments? That is, in addition to risk-free projects, suppose that certain entrepreneurs have access to investments with inframarginal returns (associated with rents to ideas, managerial skill, or market power). In this case, what is taxed are rates of cash flow in excess of the firm's discount rate for depreciation allowances. Cash flows representing inframarginal returns are taxed equivalently under the broad-based income tax and the cash-flow tax (or consumption tax). As long as the scale of inframarginal projects is limited (and entrepreneurs' project selection is optimal), the tax saving from expensing should be invested in another risk-free asset. Hence, for inframarginal projects only the return representing the risk-free rate is untaxed under the cash-flow tax or consumption tax.

What about risky investments? First, risky investments generate *ex post* high or low returns. The component of capital income that represents luck after a risky investment has been made can be treated like the inframarginal return in the foregoing example of the income tax and the cash-flow tax. Second, risky investments have a higher *ex ante* required rate of return than risk-free investments, reflecting a risk premium to compensate savers for bearing risk. Whether either tax system levies a tax on the risk premium depends on how one defines a *tax*. If a tax is defined as an increase in expected government revenue, then both the income tax and the cash-flow tax include the risk premium. If, in contrast, a tax is an increase in the discounted present value of government revenue, then neither tax system includes the risk premium. In either case, the central point is that the stylized income tax and consumption tax treat the return to risk taking similarly.

To summarize, what is often called the return to capital can be thought of as the sum of the risk-free return (opportunity cost), inframarginal returns (economic profits), and returns to risk taking (payment for bearing risk and luck). In contrast to the base of the consumption tax, the income tax includes the opportunity cost of capital, which equals the rate of return on a marginal riskless project.

Critical Issues for Tax Planning under the Prototype Reforms

The returns to tax planning depend on the level of tax rates and the dispersion of tax rates across investors. Higher tax rates increase the returns to arranging financial contracts to minimize taxable income. In the simple specification described above, we assumed a single tax rate for wage income and the business-level tax. The magnitude of this single tax rate depends on policy choices about revenue needs and the desired progressivity of the tax system. Either type of tax reform can be made more progressive by increasing a household-level exemption for the wage tax component of the tax system. For a given level of revenue, increasing the household exemption typically requires a higher marginal tax rate. Most proposed versions of these tax reforms include household exemptions, which would result in a lower marginal tax rate for businesses and high-income households. Because the benefits of lowering a firm's tax base are inversely related to the tax rate, these lower marginal tax rates reduce the returns to tax planning.

The variation in tax rates across entities is an important part of tax planning because differences in tax rates across investors lead to investor "clienteles" for particular financial assets. Under current tax rules, for example, interest payments are deductible for borrowers and taxable to investors. If a high-tax-rate borrower (for example, a corporation) pays interest to a low-tax-rate lender (for example, a pension fund), then aggregate tax collections fall; in contrast, if the lender has a higher tax rate than the borrower, then the interest payment increases aggregate tax revenue. Under the tax reform proposals we examine, because there are no investor-level taxes, this form of tax planning is eliminated. Foreign investors may provide an exception to this rule. If foreign governments levy residence-based taxes, then foreign investors may face taxes on income received from U.S. businesses. Tax-exempt investors (for example, nonprofit organizations and pension funds) also deserve mention. As the largest group of zero-rate investors under current tax rules, these tax-exempt investors may lose relative to other investors as the tax rate on all domestic investors falls to zero.

Even with a single marginal tax rate for businesses, effective tax rates can still vary across firms depending on the tax rules for loss-offset provisions. Under current tax rules, firms can carry current tax losses back to offset taxes

in the previous three years or carry losses forward to offset taxable income for fifteen years; however, these rules
do not adjust for the time value of money. Hence, such
rules motivate several tax planning strategies, including
leasing and some forms of corporate reorganization. Fundamental tax reforms that retain such loss-offset rules will
continue to create incentives for this form of tax planning.

Working Definition of Tax Reform

For the remainder of this volume, we use the term *fundamental tax reform* to represent tax proposals with the following characteristics:

- We assume a combination of a business-level tax
(with either cash flow or business income as the base) and
a household wage tax.
- For an income tax version of reform, we assume
that depreciation allowances are as close to economic depreciation as possible; for the consumption tax version of
reform, businesses will deduct capital expenditures.
- The business-level tax does not distinguish between debt and equity financing.
- To minimize the differences in marginal tax rates
across business entities and investments, firms will be
allowed to carry net operating losses forward with interest.
- We assume lower marginal tax rates with a single
marginal tax rate across business entities and households;
the household tax can have a personal or family exemption.

Because fundamental tax reform implies either income tax
reform or moving to a consumption tax, we will distinguish between effects on corporate finance issues that do
not depend on the choice of tax reforms and those that
differ.

3

Valuation of Existing and New Investments

T o examine effects of fundamental income tax reform and consumption tax reform on the relative
valuation of existing business investments and new
business investments, we focus on the consequences for
equity values and interest rates on debt. To anticipate,
many of the consequences of moving from the current tax
system to the flat tax arise in the switch from the current
tax system to the comprehensive business income tax.

Tax Reform and Corporate Equity Values

One negative factor for equity demand and stock prices
can be traced to the essential difference (from the business perspective) between CBIT and the flat tax—the shift
from depreciation of capital assets under the income tax
to the expensing of capital assets under the consumption
tax. Under the income tax, the effective cost per dollar of
capital goods purchased equals $ $(1 - \tau z)$, where τ is the
corporate tax rate and z is the present value of depreciation deductions for the invested dollar. Under the consumption tax, capital investment is expensed, so that z rises to
unity and the effective cost per dollar of capital goods purchased falls to $ $(1 - \tau)$. That is, one can think of invest-
ment incentives accompanying expensing as reducing the
price of a capital good. If "new capital" purchased under

11

the expensing (consumption tax) regime is otherwise the same as "old capital" in place under the depreciation (income tax) regime, the price of old capital will fall. In this sense, investment incentives reduce the stock market value of existing capital (see, for example, Auerbach and Kotlikoff 1987; Hall 1996a). At the current corporate tax rate of 35 percent, the move from current law to expensing for equipment investment would lead to a decline in equity values through this channel of about 8 percent.[8]

This simple calculation assumes that firms can, without cost, adjust their fixed-capital stocks to take advantage of changes in expected profitability or in the tax treatment of investment. Economic studies of investment have shown, however, that firms face costs of installing new capital goods, leading firms to smooth changes in their capital stocks over time. If these "adjustment costs" are high, old capital remains valuable relative to new capital, and stock prices need not fall. If adjustment costs are low, the shift to expensing per se reduces stock prices. In their review of existing studies, Hassett and Hubbard (1997) conclude that adjustment costs are relatively low, so that focusing on the changes in τ and z is sensible for estimating consequences of expensing for stock prices.

Another consideration arises from the fact that tax reform is not a switch from CBIT to the flat tax but can be thought of more realistically as switching from the current tax system to CBIT and then from CBIT to the flat tax. The move from the current tax system to CBIT would eliminate individual-level taxes on dividends and capital gains. To the extent that investor-level dividend taxes are capitalized in share prices, they reduce the value of equities (we discuss this in more detail in chapter 4). In addition, the elimination of the capital gains tax increases the return on equities and reduces effective costs of trading equities (because the capital gains tax is both a tax on equity returns and a transactions tax), thereby raising equity values.

TABLE 3–1
EFFECTS OF THE FLAT TAX REFORM ON EQUITY PRICES

Influencing Factor	Effect on Stock Prices	Effect Traceable to	
		Move to CBIT	CBIT → flat tax
Shift to expensing	Lower	No	Yes
Elimination of investor-level dividend tax	Higher or none	Yes	No
Elimination of capital gains tax	Higher	Yes	No
Reduction of tax rate on business income	Higher	Yes	Yes

SOURCE: Authors' calculations.

13

Finally, to the extent that base broadening in tax reform reduces marginal tax rates, tax reform can reduce the tax rate on business income (or business cash flow), raising the present values of aftertax returns on business investments and equity values in the short run.

Table 3–1 summarizes the effects of consumption tax reform on corporate equity values. All else being equal, the portion of tax reform associated with the move from the current tax system to the comprehensive business income tax leads to higher equity values, while the portion of the tax reform associated with the move from CBIT to the flat tax leads to lower equity values. To the extent that either component of tax reform leads to lower marginal tax rates on business income or cash flow, equity values rise in the short run, all else being equal.

Tax Reform and Corporate Interest Rates

The effect of consumption tax reform on interest rates on business debt has been the topic of considerable debate (see, for example, Feldstein 1995; Hall 1996b). We argue below that clarifying assumptions about corporate finance and capital-market equilibrium and decomposing tax reform into two steps (that is, eliminating differential income taxation and shifting the tax base from income to consumption) make analysis of the effects of tax reform on interest rates more straightforward.

The conventional explanation of the effect on interest rates of switching from the current tax system to the flat tax is that the pretax interest rate should fall (see Hall and Rabushka 1983, 1995; Hall 1996a). The intuition for this argument is as follows. Consider the switch from the current tax system to CBIT. Two features of the CBIT reform would directly affect corporate interest rates. First, taxes on interest income are eliminated. Second, interest deductibility is eliminated. In the market for business credit, the supply schedule for credit (as a function of the interest rate) and the demand schedule (as a function of the interest rate) both shift down. In the simplest story, all interest income is taxed, and all interest expenses are deducted. In a closed economy, if there is no heterogeneity in effective tax rates, the introduction of CBIT maintains the existing aftertax interest rate; that is, the pretax interest rate falls by the amount of the tax.[9] In a small open economy, integration increases desired international lending. The effect of the shift from CBIT to the flat tax on interest rates depends on the interest sensitivity of the supply of funds to the domestic business sector. If the domestic business sector is a "small open economy," the introduction of the flat tax leaves interest rates at their CBIT levels. If the supply of funds is not perfectly elastic, the higher demand for funds leads to a decline in the pretax interest rate from its pre–tax-reform level by less than the tax wedge.

What is the capital-market equilibrium in Hall's argument? One possibility is that Hall's analysis of the flat tax implicitly takes place in a setting similar to that of Stiglitz (1973), in which all investment is financed by debt at the margin, but there is inframarginal equity in the firm. If one adopts the tax capitalization model of the dividend decision (see chapter 4), moving to CBIT raises equity values but not the rate of return on equity. As long as the supply of funds is highly sensitive to the rate of return, Hall's (1996a) analysis of interest rate responses to tax reform is consistent with this equilibrium.[10]

Feldstein (1995), by contrast, argues that interest rates are likely to rise in response to a consumption tax reform. Consider first the move from the current tax system to CBIT. Equity-financed investments benefit from the elimination of the double taxation of corporate equity in the move to integration of the corporate and individual income tax systems. With regard to corporate finance, Feldstein's model implicitly differs from Hall's in two respects. First, he appears to adopt the "traditional view" of corporate dividend decisions (see chapter 4), in which integration raises equity returns but does not lead to capitalization effects. Second, he assumes that a fixed (nonzero) fraction of new investments is financed with equity. With these assumptions, the move from the current tax system raises equity returns, and the aftertax interest rate rises to maintain the capital-market equilibrium. Going from CBIT to the flat tax, expensing raises marginal equity returns and interest rates further.

Fullerton and Gordon (1983) use a computable general equilibrium model with endogenous financial behavior (calibrated to 1973 data) to simulate the effects of integrating corporate and personal income taxes. In their case in which any revenue lost from this reform is replaced by a lump-sum tax on individuals, the risk-free interest rate changes by only a few basis points relative to the equilibrium without the reform in both the short run and the long run. While the data underlying these results are dated, the findings fall squarely in the middle of the current debate—integration of the corporate and personal taxes neither substantially raises nor lowers interest rates.

Both Hall and Feldstein assume that a fixed fraction of marginal investments (zero in Hall's case and positive in Feldstein's case) is financed with equity. More generally, information and incentive problems in capital markets suggest a role for debt and equity in the capital structure (see, for example, Gertler and Hubbard 1993). Removing the double taxation of corporate equity returns would then lead to a substitution of equity for debt and gains in efficiency (see also the simulation models used in U.S. Department of the Treasury 1992).

In summary, to predict the net response of U.S. interest rates to the switch from the current tax system to the flat tax, one would need to formulate estimates of the elasticity of funds to the business sector, the extent to which dividend taxes are capitalized in equity values, and the

TABLE 3–2
EFFECTS OF THE FLAT TAX ON CORPORATE INTEREST RATES

Influencing Factor	Effect on Corporate Interest Rates	Effect Traceable to	
		Move to CBIT	CBIT → flat tax
Demand for credit			
Elimination of interest deductibility	Lower[a]	Yes	None
Shift to expensing	Higher or none[b]	None	Yes
Supply of credit			
Elimination of interest taxation	Lower[a]	Yes	None
Increase in equity returns	Higher or none[c]	Yes	None
Increased saving	Lower or none[d]	None	Yes

a. Issue: heterogeneity of rates.
b. Issue: elasticity of supply of funds to business sector.
c. Issue: dividend tax capitalization.
d. Issue: capital-market integration.
SOURCE: Authors' calculations.

substitutability of debt and equity in corporate financing decisions. Table 3–2 pulls together the various effects of a shift from the current tax system to the flat tax on U.S. pretax interest rates.

4

Business Organization and Reorganization and Financial Policy

Traditional arguments for eliminating differential capital taxation have focused on the distortions of business organizational form arising from a classical corporate income tax (see Harberger 1962, 1966).[11] By taxing corporate equity income twice, the classical corporate tax system discourages equity-financed investment by corporations. In addition, the corporate sector must earn a higher pretax rate of profit to prevent capital from flowing to the noncorporate sector. The tax distorts the allocation of resources by discouraging the use of the corporate form even when incorporation would provide nontax benefits—such as limited liability for the owners, centralized management, free transferability of interests, and continuity. Since Harberger's seminal research, more sophisticated models have been constructed to determine the costs of the economic distortions caused by the corporate income tax (see the studies reviewed in Shoven and Whalley 1992 and U.S. Department of the Treasury 1992). Harberger's original model, for example, delineated only noncorporate and corporate sectors; some researchers developed models with more sectoral detail.

More recently, models emphasizing shifts in the relative importance of corporate and noncorporate producers within an industry have suggested greater distortions under the corporate tax than suggested by earlier approaches (see Gravelle and Kotlikoff 1989). The additional cost arises because corporate and noncorporate producers within an industry possess differential advantages. Corporations may be better able to exploit scale economies, while noncorporate organizations may be better able to encourage entrepreneurial skill. Distorting the choice between these organizational forms thus means diminishing the use of scale economies as well.

The tax bias against corporate equity investment must be placed in the context of other tax considerations. When the source of corporate equity investment is retained earnings, rather than new share issues, for example, then the funds for investment are taxed at the corporate level and as capital gains to investors. At various times and in certain industries, the combination of the corporate tax rate and the effective tax rate on capital gains has been greater than, equal to, and less than the individual income tax rate on business income. In this way, differences among tax rates may reduce, eliminate, or even reverse the bias against investment by corporations. An additional mitigating factor is the use of debt finance; to the extent that corporations finance investments through debt, the relative tax advantage for noncorporate businesses is reduced.

The switch from the current tax system to the flat tax would eliminate the distortions of organizational form arising under the classical corporate income tax. This efficiency gain—which some models summarized in U.S. Department of the Treasury (1992) suggest is substantial—is accomplished, however, as a consequence of integrating the corporate and individual income tax systems. Hence the gain would materialize in fundamental income tax reform as well as in the switch to the flat tax, although the flat tax would also address the distortion in the allocation of capital between owner-occupied housing and corporate capital.

Business Reorganization

The issues in the previous section involve the choice of organizational form for a new investment and whether the tax code favors investments that are inherently more easily organized in less heavily taxed organizational forms (usually the noncorporate sector). The tax system can also affect the allocation of assets within the corporate sector by encouraging or discouraging the transfer of ownership of assets between firms. From the perspective of maximizing aggregate firm value, mergers should occur when the value of the combined firm exceeds the sum of the value of the separate firms.[12] Likewise, partial acquisitions (for example, asset sales or the reallocation of a subsidiary) increase value when the buyer has a higher value for the assets than the existing owner. Our goal in this chapter is to provide an overview of the tax issues for corporate reorganizations without delving into the details of specific tax code sections (see Scholes and Wolfson 1992 for more details); after this overview, we discuss how fundamental tax reform would change this environment.

The tax implications of business reorganizations depend on three major questions:

• Does the seller recognize a gain (loss) on the sale?
• How does the transaction affect the future tax deductions associated with the assets being sold? That is, does the buyer get to "step up" the basis of the assets for tax purposes?
• How does the transaction affect the utilization of net operating loss carryforwards of the buyer and the seller?

In general, the answers to the first two questions are related. In a so-called tax-free reorganization, the seller does not recognize a gain, but the buyer does not get to step up the basis of the assets.[13] In such transactions, the tax attributes (remaining depreciation allowances, for example) of the target assets remain the same. Therefore, future tax deductions are what would have occurred without the reorganization. Such reorganizations are usually stock transactions in which the acquiring firm pays for the assets with shares of its stock. The seller does not incur a tax liability until the shares of stock received from the buyer are sold, at which time the tax basis depends on the tax basis in the shares in the original firm.

In a taxable transaction (typically involving cash payments), the seller recognizes a gain and pays taxes on the gain. The seller can be a corporation that sells part of its assets (or shares of a subsidiary) or the shareholders in a corporation that sell their shares in a tender offer. The seller's gain depends on the difference between the purchase price and the tax basis of the assets sold. The part of this gain associated with the "recapture" of accelerated depreciation allowances is taxed as ordinary income. The portion of the gain not associated with this recapture is taxed as capital income of the seller. This tax liability of the seller is, in part, offset by future deductions that reduce the buyer's tax liability. In a taxable transaction that generates a gain, the buyer benefits from being able to increase the assets' basis to the purchase price paid. This new basis provides deductions in calculating future taxable income depending on the depreciation schedules for the different types of assets included in the acquisition.[14] Because the seller's gain is taxed when the reorganization occurs but the depreciation allowances occur in the future, however, the value of the seller's tax liability will typically exceed the present value of the buyer's tax savings from the deductions.

The difference in the seller's tax liability on the gain

and the present value of the buyer's tax savings from the step-up in the tax basis of the assets creates a "toll" for undertaking the reorganization. Firms can avoid this toll by using tax-free reorganizations or by not undertaking the transaction. Not undertaking the transaction is analogous to the lock-in effect commonly discussed for individual portfolio choice with financial assets. If the purchase price is less than the tax basis of the assets, the toll is negative, and the incentives are reversed. The size of this toll depends on the seller's unrealized gain (which also determines the step-up in basis for the buyer) and any difference in marginal tax rates across firms. If the market value of the assets equals the assets' tax basis and the firms have the same marginal tax rate, then the toll is zero. If the market value of the assets is substantially greater than their tax basis, then the toll can be large even if the firms face the same marginal tax rate. If the seller faces a higher marginal tax rate than the buyer, then the toll will be larger since the buyer's future tax reductions will offset less of the seller's current tax liability.[15]

Because statutory corporate tax rates in the United States are approximately proportional, one might be tempted to argue that the variation in marginal tax rates across firms is small. The tax treatment of losses and the presence of foreign investors, however, can create substantial heterogeneity in effective marginal tax rates within the corporate sector. Instead of paying tax refunds to firms with losses, the U.S. government allows for tax-loss carryforwards and carrybacks; however, these provisions do not adjust for the time value of money so they provide imperfect loss offsets.[16] Firms with loss carryforwards can be thought of as having a low marginal tax rate since additional current income will create a future tax liability with a present value that is less than that implied by the statutory tax rate. Firms with taxable income may have an incentive to buy firms with loss carryforwards as a way to accelerate the use of these losses.[17]

Empirical evidence in Auerbach and Reishus (1988) suggests that taxes are not a major factor in encouraging merger and acquisition activity. Because they were examining data from 1968 to 1983 when tax rules were much more generous toward mergers, Auerbach and Reishus focus on whether observed mergers have substantial tax benefits.[18] The finding that few mergers created substantial tax benefits does not necessarily imply that taxes did not discourage other mergers for which the tax costs were high. Hypothetically, one would want to consider the population of firm combinations with positive nontax benefits and calculate the tax costs (benefits) to these mergers; if the tax costs outweigh the nontax benefits, then the tax system is impeding otherwise profitable mergers.[19] As an empirical strategy, this experiment is doomed because the nontax benefits for fictitious mergers cannot be calculated and even calculating the tax costs has severe measurement error. In other research, Hayn (1989) finds that the tax attributes of mergers are significant in explaining the abnormal returns for shareholders (of both the target and the acquiring firms) associated with merger announcements; furthermore, she finds that obtaining tax-free status significantly increases the probability of success of a proposed merger. Thus, while the evidence on whether taxes significantly affect the level of merger activity is ambiguous, taxes do appear to affect the form of acquisitions.

Tax reform would greatly affect the tax incentives (disincentives) for business reorganizations. While in many instances we argue that the effects of CBIT and the flat tax are similar, this is one area in which important differences arise. Before turning to these differences, however, we highlight the similarities in the two reforms. First, by reducing the disparity in marginal tax rates across firms and investors, both reforms greatly reduce the absolute size of the tax costs or benefits of mergers. Our description of both reforms included correcting loss carryforwards and carrybacks for the time value of money. This correction plays an important role in harmonizing effective marginal tax rates across firms. Second, both reforms exclude financial transactions from the tax base. Thus transactions that take a purely financial form will not create a tax cost (or benefit) under either reform. A firm, for example, can buy the shares of another firm without tax consequences for itself or the shareholders that sell.

The differences between the two reforms arise for "real" transactions. A firm, for example, could sell part (or all) of its assets to another firm. For simplicity, we focus on the case in which the buyer and seller face the same effective marginal tax rate, as should be true for two taxable corporations when loss carryforwards accrue with interest. Under the flat tax, taxes should not enter into the firms' decisions because the buyer gets a tax deduction that exactly offsets the inclusion in the seller's tax base. Thus, selling used assets is taxed the same as selling output between businesses. Under CBIT, the reliance on depreciation allowances creates the same type of toll described under the current tax system.[20] As under the current tax system, CBIT relies on a realization principle for measuring some components of capital income. This realization principle leads to a lock-in effect for real assets with gains. The gains or losses on these assets could arise from inflation (if depreciation allowances are not indexed) or changes in market conditions. The end result is that CBIT, unlike the flat tax, may discourage some profitable mergers or affect the form of those transactions by giving firms an incentive to structure deals as financial, rather than real, transactions. While the effect on the structure of deals is similar to the effect under current rules, with CBIT the distinction is between real and financial transactions; in contrast, the main emphasis under current rules is whether the currency in the transaction is cash or stock.

In general, either reform could greatly simplify the

tax treatment of business reorganizations. The flat tax should eliminate the role of taxes in these complicated decisions. Provided that it is relatively easy for firms to structure transactions as financial activity, CBIT will also considerably reduce the tax distortions for mergers; nonetheless, even for real transactions, CBIT will reduce the tax distortions relative to current rules by reducing the heterogeneity of effective marginal tax rates.

Corporate Financial Policy

This section discusses the implications of fundamental tax reform for how firms finance their investment. We begin with a discussion of the choice between different forms of external financing—debt or equity. Taxes can also affect whether firms use internal equity markets; that is, firms' cash distribution policies can depend on taxes. We also summarize the evidence on whether taxes affect corporate financial policy. For the United States, this empirical evidence may not be particularly useful in predicting the response to fundamental tax reform because previous time-series variation in the tax code has been small relative to the magnitude of the changes predicated by the proposed reforms.[21]

The current tax system discriminates between debt and equity in corporate financial structures. The effect of the tax distortion on debt-equity ratios and on economic efficiency depends in part on the degree of substitutability of debt and equity from a nontax perspective. If, on the one hand, firms consider debt and equity to be perfect substitutes in corporate finance, taxes will affect capital structure but will have no efficiency consequences for the firm. If, on the other hand, capital structures are completely determined by nontax considerations, differential taxation leads to differences in effective tax rates on capital among firms.

The general benchmark for analysis is again the frictionless world of Modigliani and Miller (1958): with no taxation, no bankruptcy costs, and no information problems, corporate financial policy is irrelevant. With bankruptcy costs and corporate taxes, firms experience a trade-off at the margin when raising additional debt financing between an increased probability of incurring bankruptcy costs and the tax subsidy granted to debt.

In general, both corporate and individual taxes (on ordinary income and capital gains) matter for decisions about corporate capital structures. While the corporate tax code favors debt financing, the individual tax favors equity financing. Although dividends and interest income are taxed similarly in the individual tax, equity income received in the form of capital gains is taxed at a lower effective rate on account of deferral (and, in some periods, lower explicit rates).

With corporate and individual taxes, the net tax benefit to corporate financing through debt depends on individual tax rates on interest, dividends, and capital gains, the corporate tax rate, and corporate dividend policy. In particular, for an investor facing tax rates of θ on interest and dividends and c on capital gains, the relative attractiveness of debt financing over equity financing is measured at the margin by

$$(1 - \theta) - [(1 - \tau) \, d \, (1 - \theta) + (1 - d) \, (1 - c)] - b,$$

where τ is the corporate tax rate, d is the dividend payout rate, and b is the marginal bankruptcy cost. Gordon and MacKie-Mason (1990) specify b as a function of the capital structure and obtain an expression for selecting the capital structure that maximizes the net incentive for debt financing.

In the frictionless model ($b = 0$) considered by Miller (1977), when no dividends are paid ($d = 0$) and the effective tax rate on capital gains is zero ($c = 0$), the marginal investor is indifferent between bonds and equity if $\theta = \tau$. If $\theta > \tau$, the investor will invest only in equity; if $\theta < \tau$, the investor will invest only in debt. While firms' capital structures are indeterminate, the equilibrium capital structure for firms as a whole depends on individual income tax rates and the distribution of wealth across tax brackets. While the Miller model is analytically transparent, its predictions about investor clienteles and the lack of patterns in corporate capital structures are counterfactual. Generally speaking, researchers have attempted to extend the intuition by describing cross-sectional variation in the net tax incentives based on nondebt tax shields or on information incentive problems in financial contracting.

In the first research program, DeAngelo and Masulis (1980) linked nondebt tax shields with cross-sectional variation in debt policy. In their approach, the firm's effective tax rate on interest deductions at the margin depends on such nondebt tax shields as tax-loss carryforwards and investment tax credits.[22] MacKie-Mason (1990) provides some evidence in support of this cross-sectional variation.

Other sources of cross-sectional variation arise from information and incentive problems in financial contracting. Debt can discipline the moral hazard associated with equity financing (as in Jensen and Meckling 1976), although it can also lead to inefficient increases in managerial risk taking (as in Myers 1977). In such approaches, the desirability of debt financing for nontax reasons may vary across firms according to differences in the extent of asymmetric information or in the tangibility of assets being financed.

An additional source of cross-sectional variation comes from differences in firms' relative exposure to idiosyncratic and aggregate risk as in Gertler and Hubbard (1993). Even without taxes, the presence of both types of risk leads to the use of both debt and equity in corporate capital structures. Tax distortions confront firms with an *ex ante* trade-off between the costs of equity finance and the costs of increasing exposure to the macroeconomic risk that accompanies debt financing. Consistent with the model, Gertler and Hubbard show that, holding firm-level determinants of dividends constant, dividend payments rise in aggregate good times and fall in aggregate bad times.

An additional possible source of cross-sectional variation is cross-country differences in capital structure for "similarly situated" firms. Rajan and Zingales (1995) offer some suggestive evidence that cross-country differences in the net incentive for debt financing are positively associated with cross-country differences in leverage. One could extend this line of inquiry by studying differences in leverage across countries for firms in the same industry or by exploiting the cross-sectional variation in the net incentive for leverage created by major tax reforms (as in Cummins, Hassett, and Hubbard 1996 for investment).

Further empirical research is needed to examine the degree of substitutability of debt and equity in corporate capital structures and in household portfolios to refine estimated welfare gains from eliminating financing distortions. The economic models used in the Treasury Department's corporate tax integration study (U.S. Department of the Treasury 1992) suggest modest efficiency gains from eliminating corporate financing distortions. Returning to our theme, the gains from fundamental income tax reform (CBIT) and the flat tax would be identical.

Corporate Payout Policy

One significant source of tax asymmetry in corporate financial policy arises from the differential treatment at the individual level of equity income in the form of dividends and capital gains. Distributing earnings through dividends is taxed relatively highly versus distributing earnings through capital gains generated by reinvested earnings or share repurchases.

Financial economists have offered two explanations for why corporate dividends are paid despite the tax bias against dividend distributions (see, for example, the review of Poterba and Summers 1985; and U.S. Treasury Department 1992).[23] The first—known as the "traditional view"—argues that dividends offer nontax benefits to shareholders that offset their apparent tax disadvantage. Analogous to the earlier discussion of nontax benefits of debt finance, for example, high dividend payouts may decrease managerial discretion over internal funds. Alternatively, dividends may provide signals to investors about a firm's prospects or relative financial strength, although the need to maintain dividend payments as a signal will constrain the use of retained earnings as a corporation's source of financing for new investments. Under the traditional view, firms set dividend payments so that, for the last dollar of dividends paid, the incremental nontax benefit of dividends equals their incremental tax cost. Thus, the amount of dividends paid out is expected to decrease as the tax burden on dividends relative to capital gains increases.[24] The Treasury Department's integration report largely adopted this approach.

The second explanation, or "tax capitalization view," assumes that dividends offer no nontax benefits to shareholders relative to retained earnings (see Auerbach 1979; Bradford 1981; King 1977).[25] An additional assumption in this view is that corporations have no alternative to dividends (like share repurchases) for distributing funds to shareholders. As a result, investor-level taxes on dividends reduce the value of the firm (as they are capitalized in share values) but would generally affect neither corporate dividend nor investment decisions. Under the assumptions of the tax capitalization view, corporate tax integration or switching to the flat tax would not encourage corporations to increase dividend payouts but would confer a windfall on holders of existing equity.

Two types of empirical tests figure prominently in examinations of the traditional view. One approach (identified with Poterba and Summers 1985) tests the relative predictive power of a model in which marginal equity financing comes through new shares issues (in which $q = 1$, the traditional view) and a model in which retained earnings are the marginal source of equity financing (in which $q < 1$, the tax capitalization view). Poterba and Summers find that the q model based on the traditional view has greater explanatory power (although there are real concerns about measurement error in proxies for q; see Hassett and Hubbard 1997). A second line of inquiry compares the costs of paying dividends with the effect of distributions on share values. Bernheim and Wantz (1995) argue, for example, that if dividends are used to signal future prospects, their information content (effect on value) should relate to their tax cost. Bernheim and Wantz estimate that the information content per dollar of dividend distributions declined with the investor tax rate on dividends in U.S. tax reforms in 1981 and 1986, consistent with the traditional view. Such evidence is not necessarily inconsistent with the tax capitalization view if investors anticipated reductions in marginal tax rates on dividends.

The tax capitalization view confronts the problem that dividends appear to be smoothed relative to fluctuations in fixed investment spending.[26] Auerbach and Hassett (1996) observe that if dividends are more costly for firms to adjust than capital structure, then dividends might fall when improvements in investment opportunities increase investment demand. That is, while dividends eventually rise in response to the higher profitability, they may fall in the short run to fund investment. Using Compustat data and a measure of q to control for investment opportunities, they find that an increase in a firm's investment rates reduces dividend payouts, while an increase in cash flow increases payout. While the Auerbach-Hassett results are suggestive, the authors do not consider the more general model of different adjustment costs for fixed investment, dividend payout, capital structure, and liquidity.

TABLE 4–1
EFFECT OF THE FLAT TAX ON BUSINESS ORGANIZATION AND
FINANCING DECISIONS

		Effect Traceable to	
Influencing Factor	Effect on	Move to CBIT	CBIT→ flat tax
Organizational form			
Elimination of classical corporate income tax	Corporate versus non-corporate form	Yes	No
Elimination of lock-in for business assets in reorganizations	Financial transactions	Yes	No
	Real transactions	No	Yes
Capital structure			
Elimination of tax distinction between debt and equity	Corporate capital structure	Yes	No
Elimination of distinction between retentions and distributions	Corporate payout policy	Yes	No

SOURCE: Authors' calculations.

Summary

Table 4–1 summarizes the consequences of flat tax reform for business organization and reorganization, capital structure, and payout policy. In most cases, the salutary consequences of tax reform can be traced to gains from the switch from the current tax system to the comprehensive business income tax.

5
Tax Planning
after Tax Reform

The issues of organizational form and financial structure are corporate tax-planning decisions at a very broad level. Tax planning, however, has another, more microlevel, dimension of affecting issues such as security design and the hedging of risk. In its extreme form, this tax planning leads to tax arbitrage—investments in which firms have a zero net position but earn income from the differential taxation of the components of the transaction.

This chapter outlines how tax reform attacks the underlying concepts that create tax-planning opportunities under current law. We then discuss specific examples of how tax reform would impede particular financial transactions for avoiding taxes. Instead of providing an exhaustive list of tax avoidance strategies, we focus on stylized examples to give a flavor of how tax reform would change financial planning. While the economics and finance literature has long recognized the role of complex financial instruments in tax avoidance, the details of particular transactions are much more developed in the tax law literature.[27] We conclude the chapter by speculating on some potential tax-planning techniques that would become more prominent after fundamental tax reform.

Motives for Tax Planning

Tax rate differentials—across investors and across different types of income—play a crucial role in tax planning. The simplest tax rate differentials occur across investors. Some investors face higher marginal tax rates than other investors. With progressive tax rates, for example, marginal tax rates on income rise with income. Another major differential exists between taxable investors and tax-exempt investors, such as pension funds and not-for-profit organizations. Often, these differentials reflect policy decisions that tax rates should vary depending on the ownership of income. By themselves, these tax rate differentials across investors create incentives for investors with positive income to try for a lower tax rate classification and investors with negative income to try for a higher classification. Parents (corporations) with high marginal tax rates, for example, may try to shift income to their children (unconsolidated subsidiaries or pension funds) who face a lower marginal tax rate.

Stronger tax incentives occur when these tax rate differentials across investors are combined with tax differences across types of assets or income. The current tax system has a myriad of distinctions among types of income. Income can be either ordinary (wages, interest, or dividends, for example) or capital (capital gains, for instance). Notice that "capital" refers to whether income is taxed on realization or accrual rather than whether the source of income is capital or labor. Tax rates differ across income types for individuals who face lower tax rates on capital gains than on ordinary income. The timing of tax payments may also differ because capital income is taxed on realization rather than accrual. We discussed the implications of the distinction between dividends and capital gains income for corporate payout policy in chapter 4. The distinction between debt and equity provides another tax rate differential. The tax code differentiates between debt and equity at both the firm and the investor level. At the firm level, equity-financed investment is taxed more heavily than debt-financed investment since interest payments are deductible; however, the reverse is typically true for investors, because equity investments offer opportunities for deferral. Variation in tax rates by type of income creates incentives for investors to attempt to recharacterize income from highly taxed forms to lightly taxed forms.

Combining these two types of tax incentives creates clientele-based tax-planning opportunities. Investors with high tax rates are the natural clientele for lightly taxed forms of income (high-tax-rate investors, for example, own municipal bonds) and investors with low tax rates tend toward highly taxed assets (pension funds, for example, own corporate bonds). The flexibility inherent in financial assets facilitates splitting the returns on real assets to construct these clienteles.

The current tax system specifies rules for the taxation of different types of assets. Examples include the depreciation schedules for cost recovery on physical assets, rules to differentiate equity from debt, and rules applying to original issue debt to determine the accrual of interest income and deductions. While many of these rules must inherently rely on arbitrary judgments, the rules for financial transactions are difficult to design because a set of cash flows can be produced by many different financial arrangements. Unless all these arrangements yield the same tax result, then firms and individuals have an incentive to choose the financial arrangements that minimize their tax burdens. Financial markets have developed derivative securities and other complex transactions that make it difficult to trace what it means to own a particular asset. The risk involved in owning a share of stock, for example, can be undone by either selling the share, short-selling the share, or writing an appropriate set of options on the share; however, these three methods of disposing of risk are taxed differently.[28] These differences in the taxation of economically similar transactions create arbitrage opportunities. Because the principal role of financial markets is to make financial claims liquid and fungible, it is inherently difficult to measure consistently the outcomes of these different transactions (see, for example, Weisbach 1995). For physical assets, however, it is relatively easy to assign ownership of the asset to an entity and measure the benefits and costs of ownership.[29]

One of the most radical features of fundamental tax reform is its shift in the types of transactions subject to the tax system. The current income tax base includes both "real" and "financial" transactions. Measuring corporate income as a proxy for the return on the productive assets of the firm, for example, is an exercise in taxing real transactions, whereas measuring the returns on the debt and equity contracts financing this investment focuses on a set of financial transactions. Neither CBIT nor the flat tax would attempt to tax financial transactions; instead, these tax systems focus on taxing real transactions by businesses and households. CBIT would measure the capital income of businesses and the labor income of households; the flat tax would levy a cash-flow tax on businesses and a labor income tax on households. Financial transactions between businesses, between households, or between a business and a household would not be targets of the tax system.

Excluding financial transactions from the tax base is not necessarily a feature of fundamental tax reform. Alternative integration proposals, such as dividend deduction or imputation systems, would continue to base the tax system on a combination of real and financial transactions. Consumption tax proposals based on the personal expenditure model would also tax a combination of real and financial transactions. Thus, the advantages and disadvantages of focusing the tax system on real transactions are specific to the proposals we outlined as prototypes for reform rather than being generic features of moving to a pure income or consumption tax.

Fundamental tax reform dramatically reduces the incentives for tax planning. This reduction comes primarily from reducing the disparity in tax rates for various types of transactions. Under either the flat tax or CBIT, for example, investors in financial assets face a marginal tax rate of zero. In addition, issuers of financial assets do not get deductions from their tax bases for returns paid on different financial assets (interest is not deductible, for example). For real assets used for business purposes, all firms have a common marginal tax rate that applies to cash flow under the flat tax or business income under CBIT. Furthermore, allowing losses to be carried forward with interest reduces the tax rate differential between firms with positive and firms with negative tax bases. In addition, by lowering the top marginal tax rates, tax reform reduces the incentives for clientele-based tax planning even in cases when a transaction is taxed differently across investors.

By not taxing financial transactions, tax reform eliminates the tax rate differentials on ordinary and capital income and on debt and equity returns. Thus, tax reform eliminates the tax preference for different forms of finance and the incentives for forming tax clienteles in portfolio choice. As we discuss below, one difference between the two types of reform is that the flat tax is neutral between real and financial transactions but CBIT may create some tax preferences for structuring transactions as financial rather than as real.

Distinguishing Debt from Equity

As discussed in chapter 4, the double taxation of equity-financed corporate investment can affect a firm's choice between debt and equity financing. In addition, this double taxation creates incentives for financial market innovation that push the boundaries of the Treasury Department's definitions of debt and equity for tax purposes. The tax advantage of these innovations relies on the differential tax rate on equity- and debt-financed investment at the corporate level. One such innovation with growing popularity is a class of hybrid securities typified by monthly income preferred stock (MIPS). For the issuer, MIPS combines the tax deductibility of debt with many of the features of preferred stock.

The key element for achieving these tax benefits is the insertion of a financial intermediary that is not taxed as a corporation between the issuer of the security and the buyer of the security.[30] For MIPS, this intermediary is often a limited liability company (LLC) that is wholly owned by the issuer. The LLC is taxed as a partnership under U.S. tax law because it has neither continuity of life nor freely transferable ownership claims.[31] The LLC issues publicly traded preferred stock and lends the proceeds to the parent. The loan is subordinated debt, so that in bankruptcy it is junior to the parent's other debts but senior to the claims of shareholders. The parent's interest expense is tax deductible, but it creates income for the LLC. Typically, the parent's interest payments are timed to match the preferred stock dividends of the LLC.[32] Thus, the owners of the MIPS receive dividends equal to their share of the LLC's taxable income and typically pay taxes on the cash received as ordinary income.[33] For financial accounting purposes, the transaction is viewed as if the parent had issued the preferred stock because it is the sole owner of the common shares of the LLC.

Goldman Sachs developed MIPS in 1993 in an offering for Texaco. Subsequently, investment banks have embellished on the MIPS structure with various features regarding the organizational form of the "middle man," redemption options, and payment structures. Rather than organizing an LLC, which has the paperwork associated with partnership taxation, Merrill Lynch used a trust as the financial intermediary in creating trust originated preferred securities (TOPRS).[34] While in 1993 these hybrid securities accounted for just 4 percent of preferred stock issues, they grew to 52 percent of preferred stock issues in 1994 and over 70 percent of such issues in 1995 (see Crain and Jackson 1996).

For the issuer, the advantage of MIPS over traditional preferred stock is that dividends are essentially paid with pretax income rather than aftertax income. With a 35 percent corporate tax rate, for example, a corporation raising $100 million through a MIPS issue with a promised yield of 10 percent saves $3.5 million annually in tax payments relative to issuing traditional preferred stock with the same yield.[35] In practice, MIPS pays slightly higher yields (often about seventy-five basis points) than traditional preferred stock, so some of the firm's tax benefits are lost in the form of higher pretax returns to investors (see Bary 1995). It is unclear whether this difference in yields is associated with the introduction of a new financial product or will be an artifact of the long-run pricing of these securities. For individual investors, the tax treatment of preferred stock dividends and MIPS dividends is the same (provided the parent does not defer any interest payments). In addition, tax-exempt investors should be indifferent between holding MIPS and holding traditional preferred stock. Because MIPS owners include allocated income from the LLC in their tax bases (rather than dividends), however, corporate investors do not get the dividends deduction received for owning MIPS, which may lead them to prefer traditional preferred stock.

Tax Reform and MIPS

Fundamental tax reform would eliminate the need for financial innovations such as MIPS. By eliminating the distinction between debt and equity, either CBIT or the flat tax would reduce the incentives to blur the distinction between debt and equity. By reducing the amounts of tax-motivated financial "engineering," these reforms may not

greatly affect the level or composition of corporate investment; however, there could be social benefits from reducing the resources devoted to creating, marketing, and
managing these financial transactions.[36] One benefit of fundamental tax reform is the possibility of redirecting the
energies of corporate financial planning from tax planning
to other economic goals, such as the allocation of risk.

The MIPS example highlights the somewhat arbitrary
nature of deciding whether a financing tool qualifies for
the tax advantages of debt. It is easy to imagine tax regulations reclassifying MIPS as preferred stock for tax purposes rather than as debt. These targeted reforms would
have the flavor of consolidating the parent firm and the
financial intermediary (the LLC, for example) for tax purposes. These "simple" reforms, though, beg the question of
determining when the financial intermediary is sufficiently
unrelated to the parent firm so that the loan receives the
tax treatment of debt.

In general, fundamental tax reforms obviate the need
for the arbitrary distinctions between debt and equity financing arrangements. Under the current tax system, it
is unclear why the level of taxation on investment should
depend heavily on the form of financing and the arbitrary
tax rules determining the taxation of different securities.
As financial markets become even more sophisticated, the
line between debt and equity for tax purposes is likely to
be tested more often. Other recent examples of securities
that challenge the tax classification are long-maturity (fifty
or a hundred years, for example) zero-coupon bonds, contingent debt (loans with interest payments contingent on equity returns, for instance), and step-down preferred stock.[37]

Realization-based Tax Rules

In this section, we present a stylized example of how derivative securities can be used in tax planning and discuss how the prototypical reforms would affect these forms

of tax avoidance. Our example has three critical features. First, assets differ in how they are taxed. Second, tax rate differences across investors create tax-motivated clienteles for the assets. Third, derivative securities can be written on the assets without triggering a change in how the underlying assets are taxed.

A simple illustration of how taxation differs across assets is the difference between assets taxed on an accrual basis and those taxed on a realization basis. For a constant tax rate, accrual-based taxation leads to a higher tax burden than realization-based taxation, because the realization principle allows for deferral of taxes. For concreteness, we label the asset taxed on accrual as debt and the asset taxed on realization as (non–dividend-paying) equity. With these labels, the assets have obvious economic differences in terms of risk, priority in bankruptcy, and decision-making responsibilities. In some cases, these nontax differences can be quite small; however, for the tax code to treat the assets differently, the assets need at least some cosmetic nontax difference. Our example focuses on the differences in risk and assumes the other nontax motivations for holding different securities are relatively unimportant.

Tax rate differences across investors could come from a variety of sources. Progressive rates on capital income received by households provide one such source but probably not an important one for tax planning with derivative securities. Taxable businesses could face different marginal tax rates, especially given the loss offset rules of the current tax system. The simplest example of tax rate differences across investors is perhaps that between taxable investors (businesses or households) and tax-exempt investors, such as tax-exempt organizations and pension funds. The combination of the differences in tax treatment of assets and tax rates for investors creates tax-motivated clienteles for the assets. For simplicity (and without loss of generality), we consider a transaction between a tax-

able investor and a nontaxable investor. Similar calculations hold for any tax rate differential. The taxable investor prefers the lightly taxed asset, and the nontaxable
investor is the natural clientele for the heavily taxed asset.

The downside to these tax-motivated investment
strategies is that the high-tax-rate investor might not like
the nontax characteristics of the lightly taxed asset (it is
too risky, for example) and vice versa. Derivative securities offer investors a mechanism for trading the risk characteristics of the assets without giving up the tax
characteristics. As an example of a derivative security, we
use a swap contract.[38] Suppose the debt offers a riskless
return and the equity offers a risky return. For tax reasons, tax-exempt investors tilt their portfolios toward debt,
and the taxable investors increase their relative holdings
of equity. To undo this tax distortion in the riskiness of
their portfolios, the investors enter into a swap contract.
The tax-exempt investor promises to pay the taxable investor the return on a fixed amount of debt in exchange
for the return on an investment of the same-size stake in
the equity security at some specified future date (such as
five years from the beginning of the contract). The size of
the investment (that is, the fixed amount of debt specified
in the contract) is referred to as the notional principal for
the contract. Through the swap contract, the high-tax-rate
investor's exposure to the risk of the equity return falls,
and the tax-exempt investor's exposure to this risk increases. This contract is taxed on a cash-flow basis, however, rather than on an accrual basis.

At the end of the contract, if the equity has outper-
formed the debt, then the taxable investor pays the tax-
exempt investor the value of the equity return in excess of
the return on debt.[39] This payment would decrease the taxable investor's taxable income and increase the tax base
of the counterparty (not relevant in the case of the tax-
exempt investor).[40] The taxable investor has hedged the
risk of owning the equity, replacing the risky return with

the safe return on debt. The taxation of this safe return, however, is deferred until the settlement of the swap contract. Effectively, the taxable investor has recharacterized the financial return on debt from being taxed on accrual to being taxed on realization.

These tax avoidance strategies are even more powerful when the owner of the equity has an unrealized capital gain. The swap contract allows the investor to hedge the risk of future price changes but continue to defer the tax on the gain. Without these derivative securities, the unrealized capital gain creates the well-known "lock-in" effect of discouraging portfolio reallocation. The derivative securities allow investors to sidestep the lock-in effect: the derivative security can hedge all (or, at the investor's discretion, some) of the risk of keeping the asset with gain, but its use does not trigger a tax on the unrealized gain. Of course, for many investors, the transaction costs of this type of tax planning are prohibitively expensive; however, as liquidity in these financial markets improves, the costs of these strategies may fall considerably.

Tax reform greatly reduces the scope for tax planning through derivative securities. Both CBIT and the flat tax eliminate the critical elements of these strategies— the disparity in tax rates across assets and across investors. For both the issuer and the investor, debt and equity have symmetric treatment. For financial investments, both reforms have zero marginal tax rates for all investors. Thus, investors can reallocate their portfolios without triggering realization-based taxes.

New Frontiers in Tax Planning

While these prototypical tax reforms eliminate the distinctions between debt and equity and the tax status of many business organizational forms, they rely on separating business transactions into "real" and "financial" categories. It is natural to ask whether reliance on this classification will create a new genre of tax-planning techniques. For many transactions, such as the purchase of a printing press or a bank loan, the classification seems incorruptible. Tax planning, however, can require devising complex legal transactions to accomplish simple goals. To fix ideas, we examine a stylized case of the tax treatment of the sale of an intangible asset under the flat tax and CBIT. We also briefly review the challenges created by financial intermediaries for tax reform that have been discussed in more detail elsewhere (see Bradford 1996).

One area in which the distinction between real and financial transactions can become blurred is the creation of intangible capital, such as the transfer of a new technology. For simplicity, consider a small research firm owned by an inventor. The firm has expertise in research but not in manufacturing, so it plans to sell its research output to other firms. The firm produces a new invention with a market value far beyond the research cost. To ensure that the inventor receives the rewards of the invention, we assume that the new technology cannot be replicated by other firms. If this new technology is embodied in a piece of tangible equipment, then selling the invention would obviously fit the definition of a "real" transaction. Under a consumption tax version of tax reform, this transaction increases the tax base of the inventor and decreases the tax base of the buyer by equal amounts. Under an income tax reform, this transaction increases the tax base of the inventor by the sales price but because the buyer depreciates the machinery, the present value of the buyer's tax base falls by less than the purchase price of the machine.

The distinction between real and financial transactions is less clear if the invention is protected by a patent rather than being embodied in physical capital. The question becomes whether selling the patent is a real or a financial transaction. If it is a real transaction, then the tax treatment is identical to the sale of a machine; if it is a financial transaction, then the sales price would not be included in the tax base of the seller or give rise to deductions for the buyer. The seller would prefer to label the transaction as "financial" to avoid including it as taxable income, but the buyer would prefer to label it as a "real" transaction to generate deductions (either immediately under a consumption tax or over time under an income tax). Therefore, the first rule for eliminating this tax avoidance scheme is to force the buyer and seller to treat the transaction symmetrically.

The choice of whether the transaction is real or financial would greatly affect the price of the patent—the pretax price of a real transaction will be higher than the price in a financial transaction (in which the pretax price equals the aftertax price) because a real transaction reduces the tax liability of the buyer but increases the tax liability of the seller. Under a consumption tax, assuming the buyer and seller face the same marginal tax rate, the decreased tax liability of the buyer exactly offsets the increased tax liability of the seller. Thus, the parties should be indifferent to whether the transaction is classified real or financial. For an income tax, treating the transaction as financial may lower the total tax liabilities of the buyer and seller because the buyer would get deductions only over the life of the patent rather than at the time of purchase. That is, the income tax will levy a tax on the time value of waiting for these depreciation allowances by collecting tax from the seller but reducing the buyer's tax base only over time.

Because under an income tax the tax revenue generated by this transaction depends on whether it is treated as a real or as a financial transaction, the tax code would need rules, such as amortization schedules based on the projected life of a patent, for determining the tax treatment of a transaction. Tax planning, however, sometimes involves pushing the limits of regulations. Rather than purchase the patent and take tax deductions according to the amortization schedule, for example, the acquiring firm could buy all the equity of the firm that owns the patent.[41] By selling equity rather than the patent, the purchase price is not included in the seller's tax base. After the merger, the buyer could use the patent and would be allowed tax deductions associated with the new business; however, the buyer would not get depreciation allowances for tax purposes for the entire purchase price of the business. Given the time value of money, the present value of the reduction in the seller's tax liability should exceed the present value of any additional taxes paid by the buyer created by opting for a financial transaction rather than a real transaction. This example highlights the ability of businesses to structure transactions as the transfer of either real or financial assets depending on which provides the better tax result. Provided that the transaction is between two businesses with the same tax rate, this form of tax planning is effective under CBIT but not under the flat tax, because the firms should be indifferent to the distinction between real and financial transactions under the flat tax.

If the businesses do not have the same tax rate or one party to the transaction is a household, then the distinction between real and financial transactions can create tax-planning opportunities even under the flat tax. For a transaction between a business and a household, the tax base of the business includes cash received for real transactions (the sale of goods or services) but not the proceeds from financial transactions (proceeds from borrowing or interest received); neither type of transaction creates a deduction from the household's tax base. Thus, in the extreme, the tax incentives are for a household to buy grocery stores and consume the inventory instead of buying groceries. A more realistic example, as discussed by McLure and Zodrow (1996), involves dividing a household's payment for durable consumption goods into the purchase price of the good (included in the seller's tax base) and the interest on a loan (not included in the seller's tax base).[42] The general tax avoidance issue, applicable in some degree to the current system, is whether a business can transfer consumption to its owners (or employees) without that consumption's being measured appropriately by the tax system.[43]

Tax planning that uses (or abuses) the distinction between real and financial transactions may be especially acute for financial services because the firm's "real" product (financial services) is inexorably linked to financial transactions. Bradford (1996) discusses the difficulties of taxing financial services. He concludes that the problems of taxing the financial service industry are not particular to either type of tax system. Some types of tax reforms (especially those similar to a value-added tax, as would be the case for either the flat tax or CBIT), however, raise the political profile of these problems. In addition, for transactions between businesses, provided the two firms face the same marginal tax rate, the tax treatment of financial intermediation is of relatively minor importance. This conclusion follows from the same type of arguments we described above for why the choice of treating the sale of a patent under the flat tax as a real and financial transaction does not affect the total tax liability placed on the transaction.[44] Thus, the issue for financial services becomes mainly an issue of measuring household consumption.

Summary

Fundamental tax reform, as represented by either CBIT or the flat tax, could potentially uproot many of the standard corporate tax-planning techniques. These reforms lead to a more consistent and symmetric treatment of various financial transactions. Quantifying the equity and efficiency gains from these changes is a daunting task because the associated distortions arise in areas that are difficult to measure, such as risk characteristics of portfolios and transaction costs in financial markets. We conclude this chapter with two cautionary notes. First, while tax reforms promise to reduce known tax-planning techniques, some latitude would still exist for tax avoidance (especially in distinguishing real and financial transactions), and tax lawyers can be ingenious in creating new methods (see, for example, Feld 1995 and Ginsburg 1995). Second, our discussion has focused on the benefits of tax reform when tax rates are constant over time; the transition to this regime (or future changes in tax rates) might create opportunities for tax avoidance that could result in costly losses of tax revenues.

6
Conclusion

Discussion of "fundamental tax reform" by policy makers—and sometimes by economists—often treats income tax reform and consumption tax reform as polar opposites. In this volume, we evaluate consequences of tax reform on corporate finance—business organizational, financing, and tax-planning activities—to distinguish between effects of income tax reform and those of consumption tax reform. We focus on one fundamental income tax reform proposal—the Treasury Department's comprehensive business income tax—and one consumption tax reform proposal—the flat tax.

Our principal conclusions are four. First, relative to CBIT, the flat tax exempts only the risk-free return to capital; the two taxes treat similarly returns arising from risk bearing, luck, or economic rents. Second, the effect of fundamental tax reform on interest rates depends on whether dividend taxes are capitalized in share values and on the elasticity of the supply of funds to the domestic business sector with respect to the net return. Third, effects of tax reform on organization and financing decisions stem from income tax reform, although the flat tax permits simpler rules for mergers and acquisitions than CBIT. Finally, with regard to financial innovation for tax planning, to the extent that such innovations arise to muddle the distinction between debt and equity for tax purposes, they are no longer necessary under either CBIT or the flat tax. One difference between the two types of reform is that the flat tax is neutral between real and financial transactions, while CBIT may create some tax motivations for structuring merger and acquisition transactions as financial rather than real.

Our analysis has implications for the policy debate over tax reform and for economic research. Because fundamental income tax reform and consumption tax reform have broadly similar effects on many business decisions, policy makers should not consider the reforms in opposition to one another. For economists, obtaining quantitative estimates of the effects of either reform on business investment, organizational, and financing decisions and of efficiency gains requires more robust conclusions about the effect of dividend taxes on share prices, the elasticity of the supply of funds to the domestic business sector, and the substitutability of debt and equity in capital structures. These questions are, of course, not new, but they remain important topics for research in measuring gains from fundamental tax reform. In addition, more research on transition questions should shed light on such consequences of tax reform as the speed with which debt and equity contracts can be renegotiated and the extent to which anticipated future changes in tax rates cause significant tax-planning distortions.

Notes

1. In this regard, this volume extends our comparison of broad-based income taxes and consumption taxes in the taxation of capital income, where we argue that the two bases differ only in the taxation of opportunity cost returns and not in the taxation of risk, luck, or economic rents (see Gentry and Hubbard 1997).

2. As with a consumption tax, this raises questions about how to tax financial intermediaries. For suggestions, see U.S. Department of the Treasury (1992, chapter 5) and Bradford (1996).

3. Moving beyond the business sector, an important distinction between a pure income tax (sometimes referred to as a "Haig-Simons" income tax) and the combination of CBIT and a wage tax is that CBIT does not tax capital income earned outside of business entities. Owner-occupied housing is the primary form of capital outside the reach of the CBIT system. While this distinction is important for analyzing the efficiency of tax reform proposals (for instance, the allocation of capital between housing and business uses) and the distribution of tax payments, it is less clear that this omission from the tax base greatly affects the corporate finance issues surrounding tax reform.

4. If the household and business tax rates differ, then tax-planning opportunities arise from recharacterizing income as wage or capital income. This form of tax planning is especially relevant for closely held businesses that have more leeway in substituting a lightly taxed form of income for a more heavily taxed form of income. This type of tax planning is probably less relevant for publicly held corporations; however, it could create some forms of tax arbitrage for financial intermediaries.

5. Related issues arise in the discussion of consequences of other tax reform proposals. We describe other recent proposals in

Gentry and Hubbard (1997); see also Slemrod and Bakija (1996).

6. Here we are abstracting from tax loss asymmetries.

7. Life-cycle simulation models used to evaluate tax reforms follow this intuition and generally assume one risk-free return on accumulated savings (see, for example, Auerbach and Kotlikoff 1987; Hubbard and Judd 1987; Hubbard, Skinner, and Zeldes 1995; and Engen and Gale 1996). In such models, the shift from an income tax to a consumption tax is equivalent to forgiving the taxation of capital income from new saving and imposing a one-time tax on existing saving used to finance consumption.

8. Auerbach (1996) estimates that the change from the current tax system to expensing under the Hall-Rabushka flat tax would, all else being equal, reduce equity values by 5.7 percent. If transition relief is granted—in the form of allowing all existing assets to continue to receive depreciation allowances—the loss in equity values from expensing falls to 1.7 percent.

9. In reality, of course, there is heterogeneity in the effective tax rates facing suppliers and demanders of credit. For example, tax-exempt investors and lightly taxed foreign investors are major suppliers of credit to U.S. businesses.

10. Portfolio flows to the domestic business sector in response to tax reform can also affect interest rates. First, consider domestic tax-favored sectors. As of 1996, approximately 8.7 percent of outstanding debt in credit-market instruments was in the form of tax-exempt bonds. Moreover, the elimination of mortgage interest deductibility reduces the tax-favored status of owner-occupied housing. This change in tax treatment in the switch from an income tax to a consumption tax causes households to shift capital to the domestic business sector from the state and local government and housing sectors. As a result, the rise in equity returns brought about by the elimination of capital income taxes would be mitigated and with it the upward pressure on interest rates. Because the elimination of the corporate income tax eliminates the relative tax advantage of the noncorporate business sector, capital would flow from the noncorporate to the corporate sector, also mitigating the increase on aftertax corporate equity returns and reducing interest rates, all else being equal.

The international capital market adds other complications to the simple analysis of credit supply. While the polar closed-economy case we just discussed does not accurately describe contemporary capital markets, the extent to which capital is internationally mobile is the subject of rigorous debate. Available data suggest that the volume of cross-border lending in U.S. dollars is similar to borrowing by U.S. businesses. (For the end of 1994, the Bank for International Settlements estimates that cross-border claims in dollars were $2,345 billion, and Eurobonds and notes in dollars totaled $915 billion. For U.S. nonfinancial businesses, the Federal Reserve estimated credit-market borrowing to be $3,885 billion.) Hence the worldwide supply of debt to U.S. businesses may be quite responsive to changes in returns.

Ascertaining the extent to which portfolio debt capital is internationally mobile is important for assessing the response of U.S. interest rates to a switch from an income tax to a consumption tax. Suppose, for example, the reduction in demand for debt capital by the U.S. state and local government and housing sectors put downward pressure on domestic interest rates. All else being equal, there would be an outflow of debt capital from the United States to the international capital market. Foreign debt investors are not made better off under the consumption tax: No withholding tax is currently paid on portfolio interest and, because of interest deductibility, returns on debt escape tax at the corporate level. If portfolio debt capital were perfectly internationally mobile, U.S. interest rates would not decline in response to shifting capital out of the state and local government and housing sectors.

11. Because of our emphasis on corporate finance, we abstract from a more general discussion of intersectoral and interasset distortions caused by the current system of differential taxation of business capital income (see, for example, Gravelle 1981; Fullerton and Henderson 1987; and Auerbach 1989). For the most part, removing such distortions can be accomplished by fundamental income tax reform in the form of CBIT (or the spirit of the Tax Reform Act of 1986). Some additional improvements in allocational efficiency are made possible by a consumption tax because of inflation nonneutralities in the income tax (see Cohen, Hassett, and Hubbard 1997).

12. Whether maximizing aggregate firm value enhances economic welfare depends on the source of the benefits from the merger. For mergers that increase market power, the increased firm value may be more than offset by decreases in consumer surplus. Given our emphasis on corporate finance issues, we concentrate on how taxes distort merger and acquisition behavior from the firms' perspective. None of the current tax incentives or disincentives for business reorganizations can be construed as forms of corrective taxation to encourage socially productive mergers and discourage welfare-reducing mergers.

13. The term *tax-free* is somewhat misleading. In these trans-

actions, the seller does not incur a current tax liability, but the buyer may have higher future tax liabilities under a "tax-free" transaction than it would in a taxable reorganization. Thus the label "tax-free" comes from focusing narrowly on the current tax situation of the seller, rather than considering both parties of the transaction and the present value of all tax payments created by the transaction.

14. The buyer will attribute the purchase price to different assets based on estimates of the market value of the assets. The purchase price, however, may be split between buildings and equipment. The portion of the price allocated to each type of asset is depreciated following the appropriate schedule. If the purchase price exceeds the value of the specific assets, then the transaction creates goodwill, which is typically amortized using a fifteen-year life.

15. Unequal marginal tax rates complicate the analysis since they also imply that the income produced by the asset faces a different tax rate after the merger. These tax rate differences can affect the price the buyer is willing to pay in the acquisition; for example, a firm with a low tax rate may be willing to pay more for an asset than a potential buyer with a higher tax rate (conditional on the pretax income from the asset being the same regardless of which firm buys the asset).

16. Auerbach and Poterba (1987) and Altshuler and Auerbach (1990) discuss the general issues of how tax loss rules affect investment incentives; Graham (1996) presents evidence on the heterogeneity in corporate marginal tax rates.

17. Elaborate tax rules are designed to prevent trafficking in net operating loss carryforwards. Nonetheless, the general point of the treatment of losses' creating variation in tax rates remains true.

18. The major difference in tax rules for mergers before and after 1986 is the repeal of the general utilities doctrine. Before 1986, corporate liquidations would not trigger a corporate-level capital gains tax, and the liquidating dividend qualified for preferential capital gains tax rates at the shareholder level. After 1986, corporate liquidations created both a corporate-level and a shareholder-level tax.

19. Conversely, and more in the spirit of the pre-1986 data studied by Auerbach and Reishus, one could ask whether the tax benefits of some mergers were large enough to outweigh their nontax costs. In such cases, taxes would be the marginal motivation for otherwise unprofitable mergers.

20. This distortion is not caused by choosing income as the tax base. Theoretically, an income tax can be administered without the use of depreciation allowances. Instead of a preset schedule of de-

ductions, firms would periodically (annually) state the market value of their existing assets. Any decrease in the market value of assets could be deducted from the tax base, and any increase would be included in the tax base. Thus, depreciation allowances would be replaced by a "mark-to-market" system for real assets. As emphasized by Bradford (1986), it is difficult to imagine an income tax system that does not rely on transactions to measure income. This system is obviously impractical since it requires periodic asset valuation for nontraded assets. In a sense, the distortion retained by CBIT is related to the point that an income tax, unlike a consumption tax, levies a tax on the opportunity cost of capital (return to waiting). Under CBIT, this return to waiting is captured by the time value of depreciation allowances. When these allowances misforecast the future value of an asset, the distortion can arise. Suppose the asset value is higher than expected. A pure Haig-Simons income tax would record this higher than expected value as income (or as a smaller decrease in income) and, in subsequent periods, attempt to tax the return to waiting based on this new higher value of wealth. By relying on actual transactions to value assets, CBIT allows taxpayers the option of postponing the recognition of increases in wealth and postponing (relative to the theoretical benchmark) the payment of taxes.

21. Moreover, while cross-sectional differences in tax incentives can be useful in some contexts, cross-sectional variation might not be helpful in understanding how capital market equilibriums will change due to fundamental tax reform.

22. Strictly speaking, this approach depends on the cross-sectional variation's being exogenous. This is a strong requirement; one firm may have more investment tax credits than a "similar firm," because it has higher investment opportunities.

23. It is fair to say that the question of why distributions take the form of dividends—instead of, say, share repurchases—is an open question for research.

24. The traditional view is not represented by a single analytical model. In most implementations, the traditional view is taken to be consistent with models in which firms derive an advantage—reflected in market values—from the payment of dividends. Candidate models are those in which firms pay dividends to signal private information about profitability (see, for example, Bhattacharya 1979; Miller and Rock 1985; and Bernheim and Wantz 1995); reduce the scope for managerial discretion (see, for example, Easterbrook 1984 and Jensen 1986); or accommodate investors' "behavioral" preferences for dividends (see, for example, Shefrin and Statman 1984).

25. Studies of integration by the American Law Institute have sometimes adopted this view. American Law Institute (1989) assumed the tax capitalization view of the dividend decision, while American Law Institute (1992) generally argues the traditional view as a general description.

26. Another problem faced by the tax capitalization view is that dividend payouts appear to rise when dividend taxes fall (see, for example, Poterba 1987; and Bernheim and Wantz 1995). Such a pattern is not necessarily inconsistent with the tax capitalization view if dividend tax changes are temporary or if dividend taxes change only in concert with other changes in the taxation of capital income. Both of these concerns could potentially be addressed by focusing on corporate tax integration experiments, which are both long lasting and focused on a change in the dividend tax rate.

27. Recent examples from the legal literature on the general issue of taxes and financial innovation include Kleinbard (1991), Shuldiner (1992), Warren (1993), Strnad (1994), and Weisbach (1995).

28. In this example, we assume that investors' portfolio choices are motivated primarily by risk and return considerations rather than the other benefits (or burdens) of ownership, such as voting and liability issues. Paul (1996) discusses the distinction between holding (versus disposing) of an asset for tax purposes and hedging risk as a substitute for disposing of the asset.

29. While it is relatively easier to assign ownership to the returns to physical assets than the returns to financial assets, some scope still remains for tax planning with physical assets. Equipment or commercial real estate leases provide opportunities to separate the physical use of an asset from its ownership for tax purposes. As discussed below, however, the incentives for this tax planning are linked to disparities in marginal tax rates, which tax reform would reduce.

30. Crain and Jackson (1996) present an overview of the tax and financial accounting implications of MIPS; Akselrad and Bernstein (1994) discuss the tax rules surrounding MIPS.

31. A business is subject to the U.S. corporate tax if it has at least three of the following characteristics: (1) limited liability; (2) centralized management; (3) freely transferable ownership claims; and (4) continuity of life.

32. The parent firm often has the right to defer interest payments. During such periods, the LLC can suspend the payment of dividends but still accrues income interest. As a pass-through entity for tax purposes, the owners (in this case, the owners of pre-

ferred shares) of the LLC recognize income for tax purposes regardless of the cash flows.

33. If the parent has deferred interest payments, then the MIPS holder will pay taxes before the receipt of cash dividends. In contrast, with traditional preferred stock, if the issuer skips a dividend, the investor does not have a tax liability.

34. Other examples include Lehman Brothers' quarterly income capital securities (QUICS) and Goldman Sachs's quarterly income preferred securities (QUIPS). QUICS are closer to straight debt than the other securities and do not necessarily require a financial intermediary between the issuer and buyer; however, unlike standard debt, the issuer has the right to defer payments for up to five years (see Perlmuth 1995).

35. To make the $10 million annual dividend payments on traditional preferred stock, the firm needs to earn $15.38 million in pretax income and pay $5.38 million in income taxes. If the firm issues MIPS, then it deducts the $10 million payment from income; for the same $15.38 million in earnings (before interest deductions), the firm would pay tax of only $1.88 million (35 percent of $5.38 million) for a tax savings of $3.5 million. This example holds the firm's investment decision fixed; alternatively, if less heavily taxed equity is available, the firm may invest more, which would lower the marginal return to capital.

36. Measuring the social benefits from reducing these activities would be quixotic, but anecdotal evidence suggests these activities are expensive. In June 1995, RJR Nabisco offered to exchange $1.25 billion of outstanding 9.25 percent preferred stock for a 10 percent issue of TOPRS (the Merrill Lynch equivalent to MIPS). RJR paid fees totaling $20 million in part to convince investors to swap into a new product; this marketing effort included mailings of Nabisco snack packs. These payments, however, were worthwhile for RJR; accounting for the tax savings and higher yield on the TOPRS, the firm saved $26 million in 1996 with similar benefits expected in future years; see McConville (1996) for details.

37. In "step-down" preferred stock deals, companies set up real estate investment trusts to which they arrange to pay tax-deductible interest. The trusts, which are legally entitled to take a tax deduction for the dividends they pay, are then used to pay dividends to investors, generally tax-exempt organizations.

38. The swap contract is convenient for expositional purposes. One can design similar strategies by combining put and call options or forward contracts. In a description of the strategies with options, it is necessary to keep track of the exercise prices of the different

options and the tax treatment of the premiums in addition to the cash flows at settlement.

39. Contracts settle on a net basis rather than each party making a gross payment to the other.

40. In this example, we focus on how derivatives change the risk exposures of portfolios and the timing of tax liabilities. There are also issues over whether the income is classified as capital or ordinary for tax purposes.

41. Alternatively, the firm with the patent could create a subsidiary that owns the patent and sell the shares of the subsidiary to the acquirer. While the government could reclassify sham transactions, our objective here is to give an idea of how tax advisers will take advantage of tax reform.

42. McLure and Zodrow argue that these types of tax avoidance schemes might be so difficult to monitor that consumption tax reform could be better implemented under what they call a "hybrid" consumption tax. Under this hybrid, households would face a tax base similar to the flat tax (that is, financial transactions are excluded from the tax base), but the business-level tax base would include both real and financial transactions. This proposal would maintain the neutrality between debt and equity finance by including all proceeds from raising capital in the tax base of the firm and allowing the firm deductions for all disbursements on financial contracts (returns of capital, principal, interest, and dividends).

43. For a discussion of this type of tax avoidance under the current hybrid income tax, see Clotfelter (1983) and Bradford (1986).

44. Because financial services are not durable (that is, they would not need to be depreciated as an input to production), this conclusion holds for CBIT as well as the flat tax.

References

Akselrad, Ira, and Robert S. Bernstein. 1994. "MIPS and EPICS: New Debt-flavored Equity Instruments." *Journal of Corporate Taxation* (Autumn): 283–90.

Altshuler, Rosanne, and Alan J. Auerbach. 1990. "The Significance of Tax Law Asymmetries: An Empirical Investigation." *Quarterly Journal of Economics* 105 (February): 61–86.

American Law Institute, Federal Income Tax Project. 1989. *Reporter's Study Draft, Subchapter C (Supplemental Study).* Philadelphia (Memorandum by William D. Andrews, Harvard Law School).

———. 1992. *Reporter's Study Draft, Integration of the Individual and Corporate Income Taxes.* Philadelphia (Memorandum by Professor Alvin C. Warren, Harvard Law School.)

Auerbach, Alan J. 1979. "Wealth Maximization and the Cost of Capital." *Quarterly Journal of Economics* 93 (August): 433–46.

———. 1989. "The Deadweight Loss from 'Non-Neutral' Capital Income Taxation." *Journal of Public Economics* 40: 1–36.

———. 1996. "Tax Reform, Capital Allocation, Efficiency, and Growth." In *Economic Effects of Fundamental Tax Reform,* edited by Henry J. Aaron and William

G. Gale. Washington, D.C.: Brookings Institution.

Auerbach, Alan J., and Kevin A. Hassett. 1996. "On the Marginal Source of Investment Funds." Mimeograph, University of California, Berkeley, December.

Auerbach, Alan J., and Laurence J. Kotlikoff. 1987. *Dynamic Fiscal Policy.* Cambridge, U.K.: Cambridge University Press.

Auerbach, Alan J., and James M. Poterba. 1987. "Tax Loss Carryforwards and Corporate Tax Incentives." In *The Effects of Taxation on Capital Accumulation,* edited by Martin Feldstein. Chicago: University of Chicago Press, pp. 305–38.

Auerbach, Alan J., and David Reishus. 1988. "The Effects of Taxation on the Merger Decision." In *Corporate Takeovers: Causes and Consequences,* edited by Alan J. Auerbach. Chicago: University of Chicago Press, pp. 157–83.

Bary, Andrew. 1995. "What a Deal: New Breed of Preferred Issues Helps Everybody but the Tax Man." *Barron's* (February 27): 17–18.

Bernheim, B. Douglas, and Adam Wantz. 1995. "A Tax-based Test of the Dividend-Signaling Hypothesis." *American Economic Review* 85 (December): 532–51.

Bhattacharya, Sudipto. 1979. "Imperfect Information, Dividend Policy, and the 'Bird in the Hand' Fallacy." *Bell Journal of Economics* 10: 259–70.

Bradford, David F. 1981. "The Incidence and Allocation Effects of a Tax on Corporate Distributions." *Journal of Public Economics* 15 (February): 1–22.

———. 1986. *Untangling the Income Tax.* Cambridge, Mass.: Harvard University Press.

———. 1996. "Treatment of Financial Services under Income and Consumption Taxes." In *Economic Effects of Fundamental Tax Reform,* edited by Henry J. Aaron and William G. Gale. Washington, D.C.: Brookings Institution.

Clotfelter, Charles T. 1983. "Tax-induced Distortions and the Business-Pleasure Borderline: The Case of Travel and Entertainment." *American Economic Review* 73: 1053–65.

Cohen, Darrel, Kevin A. Hassett, and R. Glenn Hubbard. 1997. "Inflation and the User Cost of Capital: Does Inflation Still Matter?" Mimeograph, Columbia University, January.

Crain, John L., and Gisele Jackson. 1996. "Monthly Income Preferred Securities: A New Hybrid That Combines the Best of Equity and Debt." *CPA Journal* (May): 68–71.

Cummins, Jason G., Kevin A. Hassett, and R. Glenn Hubbard. 1996. "Tax Reforms and Investment: A Cross-Country Comparison." *Journal of Public Economics* 62: 237–73.

DeAngelo, Harry, and Ronald W. Masulis. 1980. "Optimal Capital Structure under Corporate and Personal Taxation." *Journal of Financial Economics* 8: 3–29.

Easterbrook, Frank H. 1984. "Two Agency-Cost Explanations of Dividends." *American Economic Review* 74 (September): 650–59.

Engen, Eric, and William G. Gale. 1996. "The Effect of Fundamental Tax Reform on Saving." In *Economic Effects of Fundamental Tax Reform,* edited by Henry J. Aaron and William G. Gale. Washington, D.C.: Brookings Institution.

Feld, Alan L. 1995. "Living with the Flat Tax." *National Tax Journal* 48 (December): 603–17.

Feldstein, Martin. 1995. "The Effect of a Consumption Tax on the Rate of Interest." Working paper no. 5397, National Bureau of Economic Research.

Fullerton, Don, and Roger H. Gordon. 1983. "A Reexamination of Tax Distortions in General Equilibrium Models." In *Behavioral Simulation Methods in Tax Policy Analysis,* edited by Martin Feldstein. Chicago: University of Chicago Press.

Fullerton, Don, and Yolanda Henderson. 1987. "The Impact of Fundamental Tax Reform on the Allocation of Resources." In *The Effects of Taxation on Capital Accumulation,* edited by Martin Feldstein. Chicago: University of Chicago Press.

Gentry, William M., and R. Glenn Hubbard. 1997. "Distributional Implications of Introducing a Broad-based Consumption Tax." In *Tax Policy and the Economy,* vol.11, edited by James M. Poterba. Cambridge, Mass.: MIT Press.

Gertler, Mark, and R. Glenn Hubbard. 1993. "Corporate Financial Policy, Taxation, and Macroeconomic Risk." *RAND Journal of Economics* 24 (Summer): 286–303.

Ginsburg, Martin D. 1995. "Life under a Personal Consumption Tax: Some Thoughts on Working, Saving, and Consuming in Nunn-Domenici's Tax World." *National Tax Journal* 48 (December): 585–602.

Gordon, Roger H., and Jeffrey K. MacKie-Mason. 1990. "Effects of the Tax Reform Act of 1986 on Corporate Financial Policy and Organizational Form." In *Do Taxes Matter? The Impact of the Tax Reform Act of 1986,* edited by Joel B. Slemrod. Cambridge, Mass.: MIT Press, pp. 91–131.

Graham, John R. 1996. "Proxies for the Corporate Marginal Tax Rate." *Journal of Financial Economics* 42: 187–221.

Gravelle, Jane G. 1981. "The Social Cost of the Non-Neutral Taxation: Estimates for Nonresidential Capital." In *Depreciation, Inflation, and the Taxation of Income from Capital,* edited by Charles R. Hulten. Washington, D.C.: Urban Institute, pp. 238–50.

Gravelle, Jane G., and Laurence J. Kotlikoff. 1989. "The Incidence and Efficiency Costs of Corporate Taxation When Corporate and Noncorporate Firms Produce the Same Good." *Journal of Political Economy* 97 (August): 749–80.

Hall, Robert E. "The Effects of Tax Reform on Prices and Asset Values." 1996a. In *Tax Policy and the Economy,* vol. 10, edited by James M. Poterba. Cambridge, Mass.: MIT Press.

————. 1996b. "The Effects of Tax Reform on Housing." Mimeograph, Stanford University, December.

Hall, Robert E., and Alvin Rabushka. 1983. *Low Tax, Simple Tax, Flat Tax.* New York: McGraw-Hill.

————. 1995. *The Flat Tax.* 2nd ed. Palo Alto, Calif.: Hoover Institution Press.

Harberger, Arnold C. 1962. "The Incidence of the Corporation Income Tax." *Journal of Political Economy* 70 (June): 215–40.

————. 1966. "Efficiency Effects of Taxes of Income on Capital." In *Effects of the Corporation Income Tax,* edited by Marian Krzyzaniak. Detroit: Wayne State University Press, pp. 107–17.

Hassett, Kevin A., and R. Glenn Hubbard. 1997. "Tax Policy and Investment." In *Fiscal Policy: Lessons from Economic Research,* edited by Alan J. Auerbach. Cambridge, Mass.: MIT Press.

Hayn, Carla. 1989. "Tax Attributes as Determinants of Shareholder Gains in Corporate Acquisitions." *Journal of Financial Economics* 23: 121–53.

Hubbard, R. Glenn, and Kenneth L. Judd. 1987. "Social Security and Individual Welfare: Precautionary Saving, Borrowing Constraints, and the Payroll Tax." *American Economic Review* 77 (September): 630–46.

Hubbard, R. Glenn, Jonathan S. Skinner, and Stephen P. Zeldes. 1995. "Precautionary Saving and Social Insurance." *Journal of Political Economy* 103 (April): 360–99.

Jensen, Michael C. 1986. "Agency Costs of Free Cash Flow, Corporate Finance, and Takeovers." *American Economic Review* 76 (May): 323–29.

Jensen, Michael C., and William H. Meckling. 1976. "Theory of the Firm: Managerial Behavior, Agency Costs, and Ownership Structure." *Journal of Financial Economics* 3 (October): 305–60.

King, Mervyn A. 1977. *Public Policy and the Corporation.* London: Chapman and Hall.

Kleinbard, Edward. 1991. "Equity Derivative Products: Financial Innovation's Newest Challenge to the Tax System." *Texas Law Review* 69: 1319–68.

MacKie-Mason, Jeffrey K. 1990. "Do Taxes Affect Corporate Financing Decisions?" *Journal of Finance* 45 (December): 1471–94.

McConville, Daniel J. 1996. "Trading Preferred for MIPS, TOPRS and QUIPS Takes Hard Marketing." *Corporate Cashflow* 17 (February): 32, 36.

McLure, Charles, and George Zodrow. 1996. "A Hybrid Approach to the Direct Taxation of Consumption." In *Handbook of Tax Reform*, edited by Michael J. Boskin. Palo Alto, Calif.: Hoover Institution Press.

Miller, Merton H. 1977. "Debt and Taxes." *Journal of Finance* 32 (May): 261–75.

Miller, Merton, and Kevin Rock. 1985. "Dividend Policy under Asymmetric Information." *Journal of Finance* 40 (September): 1031–51.

Modigliani, Franco, and Merton H. Miller. 1958. "The Cost of Capital, Corporation Finance, and the Theory of Investment." *American Economic Review* 48 (June): 261–97.

Myers, Stewart C. 1977. "Determinants of Corporate Borrowing." *Journal of Financial Economics* 5 (November): 147–75.

Paul, Deborah L. 1996. "Another Uneasy Compromise: The Treatment of Hedging in a Realization Income Tax." *Florida Tax Review* 3: 1–50.

Perlmuth, Lyn. 1995. "Wriggling Out of Preferred." *Institutional Investor* (November): 35–36.

Poterba, James M. 1987. "Tax Policy and Corporate Saving." *Brookings Papers on Economic Activity* (2).

Poterba, James M., and Lawrence H. Summers. 1985. "The Economic Effects of Dividend Taxes." In *Recent Advances in Corporate Finance,* edited by Edward Altman and Marti Subrahmanyam. Homewood, Ill.: Richard D. Irwin, pp. 227–84.

Rajan, Raghuram, and Luigi Zingales. 1995. "What Do We Know about Capital Structure?: Some Evidence from International Data." *Journal of Finance* 50 (December): 1421–60.

Scholes, Myron S., and Mark A. Wolfson. 1992. *Taxes and Business Strategy: A Planning Approach.* Englewood Cliffs, N.J.: Prentice-Hall.

Shefrin, Hersh M., and Meir Statman. 1984. "Explaining Investor Preference for Cash Dividends." *Journal of Financial Economics* 13 (June): 253–87.

Shoven, John B., and John Whalley. 1992. *Applying General Equilibrium.* New York: Cambridge University Press.

Shuldiner, Reed. 1992. "A General Approach to the Taxation of Financial Instruments." *Texas Law Review* 71: 243-350.

Slemrod, Joel, and Jon Bakija. 1996. *Taxing Ourselves.* Cambridge, Mass.: MIT Press.

Stiglitz, Joseph E. 1973. "Taxation, Corporate Financial Policy, and the Cost of Capital." *Journal of Public*

Economics 2 (February): 1–34.

Strnad, Jeff. 1994. "Taxing New Financial Products: A Conceptual Framework." *Stanford Law Review* 46: 569–605.

U.S. Department of the Treasury. 1992. *Integration of the Individual and Corporate Tax Systems: Taxing Business Income Once.* Washington, D.C.: U.S. Government Printing Office.

Warren, Alvin. 1993. "Financial Contract Innovation and Income Tax Policy." *Harvard Law Review* 107: 460–92.

Weisbach, David A. 1995. "Tax Responses to Financial Contract Innovation." *Tax Law Review* 50: 491-539.

About the Authors

WILLIAM M. GENTRY is an assistant professor of economics and finance at the Graduate School of Business at Columbia University, where he teaches courses on microeconomics and taxation and business strategy. He is also a faculty research fellow of the National Bureau of Economic Research. Mr. Gentry has been an assistant professor at Duke University and a visiting professor at Princeton University.

R. GLENN HUBBARD is Russell L. Carson Professor of Economics and Finance, Columbia University, where he teaches courses in public economics and finance. He is also a research associate at the National Bureau of Economic Research and a visiting scholar at the American Enterprise Institute. Mr. Hubbard received his Ph.D. from Harvard University and has been a visiting professor at Harvard University and the University of Chicago. He was deputy assistant secretary of the U.S. Treasury Department from 1991 to 1992.

www.ingramcontent.com/pod-product-compliance
Lightning Source LLC
Jackson TN
JSHW011942131224
75386JS00041B/1513